MW01102112

Conversations
With the Great Mother

Book 1

Magdala Ramirez Garcia

To my beautiful sisters, Daughters,
My beautiful Grandchild
Spiritual daughters and sons
To all my beautiful people
I love you so much
I am you
Magdala

Just a note
Conversations with the Great Mother Book 1

Came into being by a recompilation of talks, songs, poems, they came through ceremonies, seminars, from school of Ascension, chats and teachings, from Priestess and even phone calls!
My spiritual Daughter Shrishti Yadav took notes for us. She is our Sacred Scribe, and it is a time to bring that recapitulation, and it will be divided in books for it is a beautiful collection that has been happening for many years.
The Book is meant to be read in a different way. Just open the book and see where it takes you.
We are so Grateful for our Sacred Scribe Shrishti, that makes this book possible, and this is so beautiful!
Thank you mijita chula!
I am you
Magdala

— Magdala Ramirez, The Golden Era Series: On Many Realms

All is love in the purity of the expression, even the acts that separates and divides.
All that you see is love, nothing else, All interconnected, all bonded into one.
Walk away from divisions or separations, for understanding will take you into the world of observance.

All is what it is, accept, don't resist, for truth will make you free, encounter the highest truth in every corner of your being
All is good, all is beautiful, live in that entrega.

There is a space, deep inside of you That recognizes the whole, it is a space of beauty, where nothing is separated

There is a space inside of you where
you can see the clarity of your being.

All is perfect, all is love
The lies are falling, let them fall,
So, the truth can be reborn again
May you live in truth.

There is a space inside of you, where
freedom resides
A place of creation, a place of love,
A place where love and
understanding flow
Stay there, in this place, make this
one your home, for in this place
The whole is contained in the one
And the one is contained in the
whole
The rainbow bridge connects all the
realms, there is nothing separated
Nothing is loose, the bridge is the
connector,
The bridge is so strong and will
remain intact
I will give eyes to see,
Ears to hear to new song.

"In the silence you shell find me
in the deepest of the silence you heart
the voice that guides you, the voice
that loves you,

in the deepest silence you remember
the true human being you have
always been,

The time has come for human beings
to embrace your original vibration
when the great mother talks to you,
she talks in vibration
it is you the one who is translating
see your relations inside of you
see how it has been that incredible
mirror where you have been living
if you have a problem with a loved
one, see them inside of you and
connect with them inside of you
though love and you will see how the
changes happen...."

"The time has come for human beings
to embrace peace, and for the people
to recognize truth inside of the self.

. What is the path of the human being? What is my uniqueness and what does it mean for me?
Truth is that your path is very unique, it is your journey in life, your purpose in life.

If you choose your path from fear, that path will take you to fear. If you choose your path through anger, it will take you to anger.

It is time to choose from love, for that path of love will take you to becoming a true human being.

Even though people are all passing through the same things, each person's perception is so unique.

You are the one who is designing your path at the same time, you know what is in that path already. It means you are seeing yourself form the future to the present.

You already know the consequence of every single choice that you make in life.
A Moment, a sacred moment when you make a choice.

And by bringing that responsibility back to the self, you can see your path much more clearly. Love has always been unconditional.

You thought love has to do with cultural belief, age, or other paradigms. But deep inside of you knew how to recognize love.

Truth is bonded with love. You are love at the same time as you are truth.

No matter where you are in life, if you are willing to see the truth with that responsibility, with the incredible force of human being that truth will take you into a path, into the highest truth available.

That truth will take you into a higher realm of your own self. When you are asking for the highest truth available for you, you must be willing to put it on.

Drop those identities that have brought you down for a very long time.

Pain was a good teacher, but light is an incredible teacher.

Your own body of light- the one that is able to conceive this new era".

— *Magdala Ramirez, The Golden Era Series: On Love*

"It is truly love that heals, it has never been time that heals....

You thought you needed to change things, in who you are or that you needed to find love. That was a lie. You have always been love. You are love!

It is love that is taking you to many, many worlds, and many encounters of yourself.

Life is a journey. And that journey takes you to many places of expressing love that you are.

All your relations are sacred, which is the incredible bonding of love that you have with that person, and that is forever, for love never ends.

*When you begin to connect within
yourself and see life through the
perception of love, immediately you
begin to increase your own power as
a human being.*

*It makes you happy, it makes you
smile. By feeling this love and being
this love all the time,
people bring forward new ways of
expression of this love like
compassion;
like the understanding of the world
of oneness and the understanding of
the interconnection within yourself,
and all around you."*

*~ Magdala Ramirez, The Golden
Series: Harnessing the Emotional
Body*

*"In this time, you are also awakening
this incredible power that is natural
for the true human being.*

*You are interconnected with everyone
and in movement with everyone. But
also, it is the power you are
embracing through that incredible
entrega.*

*So. if you feel that you need to hide
your shadow,
because that is how you have been
taught in the system and you won't
be able to transmute it- in that
moment,
you are being it.*

*At the moment you are seeing it, you
are transmuting it. Understand that
flip in your life, in your energy -*

embrace that part of you that knows how to do this.

Recognize that part of you in that incredible moment of the liberations. You know how to do this. There is a moment that all the centers in your body align with the one that created you.

Remember that you have always been the light body - hat light body, when you use it and identify with it- use it and understand that is who you are, you are not using the physical body or the programming in the physical body.

It is very much using that light body, that heart that is connected with the universe - it is using that part of you that knows how to do this."

When you remember your Being,
you also are aware about different
aspects of yourself
that are living in different time
spaces...

It is the time of integration of all
your you's the one from past present
or future or any aspect of reality
coming forward for they are just
aspects of yourself.

Time of integration.

You have the power of unity.
It is because of you that unity is
possible. Instead of looking for unity
in the outside realm, in the world of
the form.

Unity is a revelation within your
own self when you understand that
you have always been living into
world of oneness.

All connections are happening inside of you as a hologram...the reality that you are seeing is only being perceived by one aspect of yourself, and when you are able to integrate this, a great power will come to you.

Time of forgiveness.

Go into the next step...it happens naturally when you are able to comprehend that understanding that love that you are, and your mind together is able to take you into the next step of the pyramid/evolution.

Forgiveness will liberate you from the karma too...don't do the same thing again....

You know what is going on and you know your place. Recognize yourself as life.

*When you raise your vibration, you
begin to recognize that you are life.
the same life force that is in you is in
the trees... the same life force that is
in the sun...
Wake up early... and look at the
sun... he is giving you the
medicine...*

*You live in the world of light
...when you begin to feel the light in
people around you, that light will
look for unity naturally and it will
take you to the next step...*

*The transition times are important...
it might be that you feel anger ,
frustration and anxiety...
that has been part of the
programming that you are supposed
to depend on the system...
recognize the forces of racism etc.
within yourself...
once you begin to comprehend that
the major colors of the skin are
relative to the elements...*

19

those elements are inside of . . . when
you are able to see this you will
recognize unity. . .

It is the time to recognize that the
Great Mother wants all her children
in harmony and it's based on
recognizing respect, love and light
that you are searching.

In the transition times it is good for
you to remain inside your inner
home/in the presence of your own
presence. . . it will awake all the
senses you have including the belly
button that is part of your
connection...

Let it flow, for it is the dance of enlightenment,
Let it flow, for it is within you
Let it flow, for your love is your connection
Let it flow for you know where you are going
Let it flow for you are the spring that never ends,
For you have no beginning and no end, you are both at the same time

What makes the sensation of being stuck, is your emotional body,
wanting to hold onto things that are familiar,
don't be afraid and just let it flow,
remember to use your light body...

I have come here to tell you that
within yourself it is where the
liberation resides,

The holy spirit that is enlightening
your mind, bringing light into your
awareness

I am telling you that in your roots
resides your own liberation, you
don't need to become something that
you are not.

You choose to be born in a culture, in
a tradition, and with this you inherit
stories that have been in your
tradition, and at the beginning, there
was only one knowledge, a
knowledge that you are uncovering.

All is in your own DNA. all is
encoded in you, and is the time to
remember

It is the time for the human beings to realize that it is in your culture that you heal yourself.

It is not about becoming something that you are not, it is about respecting your own tradition, for that tradition in the very beginning holds the answer to that union of polarities understanding.

I have seen in every tradition in the world same symbols that is talking about this very, very ancient knowledge and that ancient knowledge is one.

One source of the true human being and it has been translated into many traditions and religions everywhere in the world.

The divine feminine has not come here to destroy any religion or tradition but to consummate them.

What does it mean to consummate religion?
To understand it at this time, means going into the very beginning of your beautiful traditions and understand where it was pointing what was the message and how in some way it translated into different traditions.

Yet they all come from the same source.
It is the time to comprehend that human beings have been in this beautiful planet for many, many civilizations,
and many dimensions too, the knowledge is one, and now, you are bringing back that knowledge, that talks about the true human being and the connection with the universe....

Is true that in your DNA is also so much pain and separation, stories of war and destruction, racism and separation that people have inside of their hearts for many generations, a thick layer of separation that needs to be heal, to encounter the very beginning...

It is the time to being true and that understanding is in your own DNA for that is the authentic human being,
the authentic human is in you, and in there is where resides your authenticity,

It is not about repetition from another tradition or about becoming something you are not.
That has been prevalent and has caused so much wars and destruction,
thinking that one tradition is better than the other,

one color of the skin is better than
the other.

Truth is within you, know that you
are light, that your true body is a
body of light,
that means it doesn't contain color of
skin, means you can hold into that
origin of your tradition.

The divine feminine has come in here
to remind you where is the unity
within yourself and that unity starts
with you,

In this time, it is the time of the
integration.
you have many aspects of yourself
and they are creating different lives
and experiences,
some of experiences were so painful
that you got attached to that
experience.

Is the time to revise your emotional body and begin to comprehend that there is a plane of liberation.

Don't betray yourself in any ways because every time one aspect of yourself betrays the other one, you will be creating a distortion in your unique vibration, and you are going to betray in the outside world of the form too.

That integration starts within your own self, by observing all those yous that have different belief systems and it is the time for all of them to come into a council.
The council is in you, to bring all your yous in that alignment with the one that created you in that way you are going to awake your light body, understanding the ways of the light body is understanding yourself and light.

A beautiful understanding will bring
that peace everywhere in the world
because it is that remembrance that
there has only been one knowledge.

Authenticity can be reached when
you can bring all your yous into
alignment.
that authenticity that you are you
born with is it is your right.

Truth is in your unique vibration,
you are born with it and it is so
unique and beautiful … is your true
song.

Is very powerful because that is the
key that you walk
into many worlds and dimensions.

A code is a song that you were
supposed to keep in your heart and
sing it to yourself over and over
again.

When you were little, someone told
you that you were supposed to be like
someone else.
They remove the power from you,

Maybe, they told you, you were not
good enough, that you couldn't
believe in yourself.

They told you that you need to go in
life trying to find love and you begin
to think where is that place
where I belong and
in thinking
that way you exchange many of your
tones of your original song
thinking that maybe if
you learn someone else's tradition,

if you try to fit in that you will
receive love and get a sensation of
unity.
This is a distorted way of thinking.
it is not about becoming something
you are not.

Is about embracing who you are, in there, is where that spiritual work resides and remembering who you are.

For many tribes that have never touched civilization that you call colonization, culturization-.

those beautiful tribes learned their songs and they understood and know that the beautiful planet earth provides you for the next octave of your same song in the recognition, in the knowingness that you have always been love, light that you are here to experience yourself and in this powerful times to go back into y our senses and begin to comprehend who you are and embracing yourself for who you are for real, because it is you the one that you truly need in your life.

*You must understand too, that you
have always been life,
you are eternal beings.
You are in this realm in a tiny, tiny
little time
just for you to experience yourself
and that experiencing
yourself means that you will have
different experiences in your life and
you are going to see your own
reactions and choices.*

*The moment of choice is very sacred
for it is the moment of choosing your
own authenticity or following the
mediocrity mind that was imposed.*

*When people can comprehend this, it
will create a whole new
understanding of what it means to be
a human being.*

*The eternal feminine, the feminine
principle put in your own DNA that
liberation, that unique code, that key
that only you can use to go into*

many dimensions, that vibration that you chose to be born with is a very sacred one.

*Whatever it is your tradition or your religion or your country –
it doesn't matter –
it is the same force. in the very, very essence of that because authentic vibration resides in the unity and understanding of the power that is for the authentic human being.*

*Is the time for the human beings to remember who they are and begin to respect themselves in such
a deep manner that
you don't want to become something that you are not.*

In the very beginning of your traditions, religions reside the secret of where this was hidden in your DNA.

There is no such thing as one human
being better than the other,
or one tradition better than the other.
you won't respect anyone else's
traditions if you don't respect your
own,
you cannot respect who you are, you
cannot be friends
or create a sisterhood or brotherhood
to other traditions if you cannot be
brothers and sisters to yourself,
with honor and
respect to yourself.

In that essence resides the key to
walking in dimensions.
one holds the feminine, that essence,
and the other holds the masculine,
the vibration.

You have always had that union of
polarities within you own self,
your divine masculine and feminine
have been mirroring each other
within your own self in one way or
another,

Every time you want to choose a
religion or a tradition that you have
never lived in,
you create a distortion in your own
heart instead of recognition the
wisdom of that tradition
and where it is pointing.

It is also true that in many traditions
they were able to keep it and
perpetuate it the original for a long
time in the world.

And you can see it in the ceremonies.
Is in the inside why they were
able to perpetuate such a beautiful
way of thinking.

Is the time of the unity, of the
gathering of the great integration
for in some way or another everyone
in this planet is bonded
through the whole creation, and
everything is happening within
yourself,
leaving behind the addition of the
pain and separation is passing
through the thick layer of stories
that have been separating
everyone and
is the time to hold on hands with
the one that created you so strongly
that you are able to see where your
own
tradition was point,
because those times are coming back.
you are entering
into the Golden Era.

The Golden Era, has no biases,
no pretending to be someone else.
Is through that authenticity,
because that authenticity is through
the true human being.

Maybe you have forgotten your song,
yet, it is in your heart,
it is just that you need to go through
that thick layer,
and do not be afraid.

Do not get hooked into the
experience of separation because that
is the part that the patriarchal
system wanted
to impose so badly,
and that part resides in your
emotional body
so badly thinking that
you are not good enough.

Thinking that you can't believe in
yourself, that someone else's
tradition is better than yours,
and so you think by taking
it you will be better
than someone else
and that has been a lie.

*Learning from each other is
imperative at this time, the
remembrance of how you are is very
important,
but you see it wasn't in that
tradition but in the essence of that
tradition
where this knowledge resides.*

*You know that part of respect to
yourself will bring honor in life.*

*Is part of the masculine way,
way of living, it is that respect you
have for yourself that you are able to
respect everyone tradition.*

*Is about the recognition or walking
in that truth, understanding that
whoever you are, you remember who
you are and be brave to bring your
own authenticity,*

*We have a saying in Mexico- the best
cook is the one who has their own
recipe. and this is the time you*

understand and embrace your own recipe.

It is the time where you understand and embrace your own recipe.

This means that your connection with the one that created you is direct.

There are no middle people. It is so unique that connection that it is so sacred that it can never be disturbed.

It might be that your own tradition helped you to connect in one way or the other, but it wasn't your tradition that made that makes you that connection.

For it is in every breath. it is in every instant of your being.

Is in the moment that you bring
the presence of your own presence.

When you open your senses,
all of them not just the limited senses
that the patriarchal system imposed
on you.

Open your senses in such a deep
manner that you understand the
connection that you have personally -
in that unique way of your highest
truth available.

Your connection is so unique in that
way your authenticity is being
awakened. it is the time of a great
work and that work is about
knowing yourself.

Recognizing that unique connection,
that you have with the one that
created you.

It is about understanding the unity
is not about imposing a tradition

or religion or liking for that
belonging because of your own
weakness, that unity resides
naturally.

You do live in the world of oneness,
with the whole creation.
that is the most beautiful
understanding of that unity
and is a revelation that comes
through your own authenticity,

My brother, sister, sons, daughters
is a time of a big remembrance,
the great work-
an spiritual work that it is
going to help you to
understand and embrace
who you are.

Believe in yourself.
This means that you are bringing
that holy presence to yourself.

That means that you do need YOU in
your life and remembering your song -
that beautiful understanding
of who you are.

This is the time that that human
being can see beyond the separation
but that starts within your own self.

Your own culture will heal you no
matter what you are or what you
think that you are. you all born with
that original vibration,
is the Great Mother the one who
lives in you...
is the Great Father the one that
lives THROUGH you.

One holds the essences, the other one
holds the vibration and then it is you
the one that can see one and the

same. that beautiful understanding is within your own self.

All those biases belong to that thick layer of separation thinking that in some way or another this will translate into something else that is so completely distorted.

The truth is that the only thing you have is what you have learned about yourself, what you were able to transmute within your own self you are going to do this because of love, when you are bale to understand that you have always been love you are able to communicate with these parts of yourself that are still working in those biases of separation this is the time when Human Being remember that it in yourself resides peace.

This is the time that you bring that peace forward.

There is a beautiful world
... has always been here,
Welcome to the Golden Age!
Chat talk

When people get triggered by a
trauma, it becomes an identity
instead of passing through the
trauma.
Passing through the trauma is
imperative at this time.
No one has power over you, unless
you give it to them.

As long as you are in anger, fear,
resentment, you cannot go into a
higher truth about yourself and
embrace your own ascension...

If there is some degree of separation
inside of you, something that makes
you think that you are better than
someone else, hurry up, and get rid of
that energy

A cultural belief that wants to keep everyone separated and it is your work to overcome separation within yourself.
Don't be afraid, don't give them your power anymore., bring back your power, for that energy has been keeping you a slave for many generations.

In many other countries, racism has existed in form of classism... and through your authenticity, your beautiful authentic being, you will realize that   your religion or tradition is not better than someone else's and that has been the separation imposed on the people for many, many generations....

Once that separation is being overcome you can bring the balance of the four elements within yourself...peace is not going to come forward until you bring your peace forward...

Signature of your Creator¹

The source, is your root.
That root is the very, very beginning,
the source of where you come from,
the one who created you.

The one who created you, reminds
you of your true body,
a body of light! You are a divine
spark that comes directly from
creator.

You are connection. That connection
is absolutely with everything around
you, all the life forms and inside of
you.

And that connection is creating a
beautiful bridge all around you, and
inside of you and
you become aware when you grow
through light.

Yes, you have the next octave that
Gaia provides you,
You also have a connection through
light that you are an awareness of
who you are.

The resurfacing of the original
vibration, is happening within
yourself, as you heal the
distortion of the vibration that was
created long time ago.

So much of that distortion came
through the sound, and through that
distortion, the human being began to
vibrate
in the lower vibrations that are
completely unnatural for human
beings,

Yet, the original vibration has
always been inside of
you unaltered and you have access at
any time.

Human being didn't lose their
own nature,
and it is in their nature, even when
you are being aware or not,
where the world of oneness resides,
all is to interconnect by nature,
through the essence,
where all life forms are so deeply
connected.
The perpetuation of the world of
oneness is in your own nature.

The tree, the stars are pulsating and
sending you that pulse, a wave of
information ...
you are receiving the communication
through the essence at all times...

Light comes through waves, and has
a pulsation,
Bits of information, information of
frequency and energy.

Your essence connects you to your
body of light, where you find your
own soul journey

The part of you that is impeding the higher connection is your emotional body, where attachments were created with experiences, and that created an identity.
Who you are for real is a body of light.

.... You have been here - getting the same lessons and going into the recycling bin...over and over again, until you decide another way, until you learn the lesson of the experience and don't need to repeat it again .... yet, you have been in many realms. All at the same time...

You have been everything, you have passed through almost every experience possible –
when you judge it based on cultural experience, or whatever or when you choose to be stuck in that pain... then you become fragmented...

And that creates more splits...see those experiences WITHOUT judgment,
and it will begin to create a new way of understanding...

The whole recycle bin, the slavery mentality depends on you, it is truly up to you because you have always been free, and freedom require responsibility and the awareness of your choices.

You have been choosing your experiences only based on the world of the form only. Not in the essence. Shift your awareness to the world of the essence and that will take you directly to the alignment with the one that created you.

You have a personal life that you are aware of, the family, money, work bank account at the same time you have a purpose

*in why you are here that you are
remembering
that you are part of a soul group,
you have a soul journey,*

*You have a body of light that you are
beginning to relate, beginning to
comprehend transmutation also
transcendence.*

*You are beginning to observe it so
deeply that you are beginning to see
those parts of yourself with
compassion, integrating in that way
your uniqueness and your full
memory.*

*When you want to restrict your
power and fit it into a cultural belief
then you are sending that fragmented
self back to recycle bin.*

*If you don't use the power you will
lose it, it is part of the law.*

*When it is in the inside, move the
perception of the identity you have
created about yourself.*

*When you move that identity,
forgiveness comes naturally.*

*The part of you that doesn't want to
forgive is your own ego
that still wants to perpetuate
the patriarchal system,
only an identity that holds you
down. '*

The Cloud

*When you tune into higher frequency
it protects you from the forces, dark
forces that are in the environment,
from a system, and in some way, you
might be the one that opens the door
for them.*

*When you see those energies and how
it flows through you, let them flow
and don't get identified, remember
that when you are in a sacred place it
is much easier to tune into a higher
understanding.*

*You are connecting with the natural
rhythm which is there. And reflected
in you, you are matching the rhythm
of the sun, of the earth, be in it, you
are part of the big orchestra,
you are the orchestra, you have the
signature of the one that created you,
is in your nature, a nature's
pattern...*

Your own nature, is a frequency, and is accessible for you, you tap into it over and over again, this is who you are, when you bring your identification to your own nature, your own alignment, just let it be, let it flow, and you can let it flow through you,

An understanding about where you are coming from and all the different aspects of yourself and all integrates into a higher truth when you let it flow, and that truth is so linked to the very, very center,
the source of everything and from that point you can see your life, those aspects of yourself that is your little self that doesn't mean anything, but it does.
So, if you don't judge them and let it flow it always goes back to that very center. That flowing always goes back to that source that you are and that is beautiful because you can see and feel, observe the big picture of

you, the whole thing at the same time...

When you got in here, in this realm of perception, your whole consciousness doesn't fit into your physical body, you need to have part of it and as you begin to understand, and became aware of yourself, you begin to comprehend the bigger picture, access to higher consciousness...

It is like... the cloud... do you have internet? and only you have the password... and you have all that huge consciousness that you have access anytime and it is huge because it is memories, energies, understandings, vibrations, frequency ..It is you as you ..and the only thing that you need is that awareness, knowing that you have access to a higher consciousness any time.

*Your subconscious mind and conscious
mind is linked together, there is a
place within yourself where you have
both at the same time, you have
access to "the cloud" at all times, is a
matter of frequency, you have access
to all this knowledge in some way
you are enlightening yourself...*

*So when you know that you have
access to the cloud... and then when
you clean yourself, and sometimes
that has to do with the
emotions... where clean yourself
means dropping all these emotions
that keeps you down, an identities of
lower vibrations, and might be that
has to do with the culture, or
religion, or has to do with everything
that you realize as a way of living in
a slavery understanding.*

*It might be decisions that you took
and keep on choosing those decisions
because of past experiences that*

relate an identity, a perception, experiences that you already know and is comfortable place, familiar for you, so when you really understand and embrace as just parts of you, without the attachment, you might awake this incredible compassion that will come naturally to yourself recognizing that you also have access to the cloud. You know this through your alignment.

When you ask is this happening to everyone? No. it depends on their frequency and choices in life, in their ability to let go the attachment, yet, everyone has that potentiality. It is their choice.

There are all these forces that whisper in your head and when you are not aware about it you just follow an identity because it has no ownership of yourself, so you perpetuate the same thing over and

*over again without noticing that you
are the one perpetuating it.*

*Now, why? Why was your
consciousness so limited when you
arrived in this realm?
Because is how much energy
you can hold in your body.*

*When your parents were making love
and you chose your parents as a
perfect match, it depended on how
high they can be,
how high a frequency your body can
hold or not and you mother sustained
that vibration too in some way or
another...*

*As you grown in understanding and
awareness, the frequency change, The
understanding of life change, you
know that you are life, that you are
love, that is how much you can hold
on into that body and have access to
it... you are changing your body,
training your physical body to a*

higher frequency at this time, and in
order to have access to the "cloud" it
depends on how much of that truth
you can put it on what you know..

As much as you are able to live in
that higher truth of yourself,
recognizing who you are as much
truth you can handle it
and that is how much access to the
cloud.

You can feel the presence of your
own presence and that creates
immediately that avenue of
who you are,
and it might be that presence of your
own presence has that frequency.

Frequency is very much where are
you, and will change,
and rise your consciousness
as you bring that presence and put it
on what you know.

You are what you think you are, your
identity accordingly to your
frequency, and when you "put it on
what you know", change your
frequency, and every single
knowledge every single part of it and
you can see those aspects and
teachings of how it flows in you as
you work in you.

The truth is that you are the
daughter of the Great Mother. How
much of that awareness can you put
on?

Think about Moondance and how
important this ceremony is.
First song, tell me your trouble what
has been stopping you, and then,
second song, I have decided to align
with you mama... I have decided to
align within myself, with the source,
the one that created me, ...and you
shout and sing it over and over
...and you realize that the whole
community depends on it, because it

is a co creation …. how many of the
Moondancers have been that aware
in that moment they comprehend and
align, then what happen?
For some, they were able to put it on,
… the land has been giving birth to
the many… and some they hold it,
some when they leave then they
forgot…
but as much as you go and align
with source,
as much you are
reaching yourself…

Become one with the message…
stay there…
until your whole body begins to
stabilize in a new frequency…

Think about the message you brought
to the world,
you can feel your purpose and even
put it in words that you can
understand…
calm down the parts of yourself that
are afraid of your own power,
you have the ability to put it in
words
and walk your talk…
you have the ability to enter that
revelation that comes from your
heart…

You hold hands with the one that
created you all the time, for you are
love, for you are life…
even whether or not you are
aware of it…

*The part of the human being that
still wants to create distortion or
keep on perpetuation of the
patriarchal system is in you,
and it is your job to transmute that
energy, some was inherit through
your DNA, and it created a comfort
zone...*

*That is the battle within yourself,
the part of that illusion...
at the moment you tap into your
nature in who you are...
everything in you will go back into
alignment,
you are so beautiful!
...and that is within your own
self...*

*Trusting yourself is natural,
Feeling blessed is natural
be-living is natural
Loving is natural.*

*Yes! Human beings are peaceful by
nature...*

Your Path

Put some flowers in your path
and trust that they are there...

It will come a time that the word
"trust" will be obsolete...
For it comes naturally
when you are able to put it on what
you know.

All is love in the purity of the
expression, even the acts that
separates and divide

All what you see is love, nothing else,
All interconnected, all bonded into
one.

Walk away from divisions or
separations, for understanding will
take you into the world of
observance

All is what it is, accept, don't resist,
for truth will make you free,
encounter the highest truth in every
corner of your being

All is good, all is beautiful, live in
that entrega

There is a space, deep inside of you
That recognizes the whole,
is a space of beauty, where nothing is
separated.
There is a space inside of you where
you can see the clarity of your being
All is perfect, all is love

The lies are falling, let them fall,
So, the truth can be reborn again
May you live in truth

There is a space inside of you, where
freedom resides
A place of creation, a place of love,
A place where love and
understanding flow

Stay there, in this place, make this
one your home, for in this place
The whole is contained in the one
And the one is contained in the
whole

The rainbow bridge connects all the
realms, there is nothing separated
Nothing is lost, the bridge the
connector,
The bridge is so strong and will
remain intact
I will give eyes to see,
Ears to heard to new song

I am you

Let your light be!

Let flow,
for it is the dance of enlightenment,

Let it flow,
for it is within you

Let it flow,
for your love is your connection

Let it flow
for you know where you are going

Let it flow
for you are the spring that never
ends,

For you have no begging no end,
you are both at the same time

In this time, you are awakening this incredible power that is natural for the true human being.

You are interconnected with everyone all around you and all inside of you

You are awakening the power of living with total entrega.

Yet, if you feel that you need to hide your shadow, because that is how you have been taught in the system then you won't be able to transmute it if you hide it, for in that moment, you are being it, you are judging it. In the moment that you are seeing it, you are transmuting it.

Understand that flip in your life, in your energy - embrace that part of you that knows how to do this. Recognize that part of you in that is an incredible moment of the liberations.

You know how to do this. There is a moment that all the centers in your body and aligns with the one that created you.

Remember that you have always been the light body
About the light body,
when you use it and identify with it,
you realize this is who you are,

Your heart is connected with the universe,
There is a part of you that knows how to do this."

Truth is bonded with love. You are
love at the same time as you are
truth.

No matter where you are in life,
if you are willing to see the truth
will bring responsibility,
where your liberation resides

Truth will take you into a beautiful
path,
Opening the doors to a highest truth
available.

That truth will take you into a
higher realm of your own self

...If you choose your path through
anger it will take you to anger.
It is time to choose from love,
for that path of love will take you to
becoming a true human being.

Even though you are all passing
through the same things,
each person's perception is so unique.

It is you the one who is designing
your path at the same time,
you know what is in that path
already.

It means you are seeing yourself form
the future to the present.

You already know the consequence of
every single choice that you do in life.

And by bringing that responsibility
back to the self,
you can see your path much more
clearly.

"It is truly love that heals,
it has never been time that heals....

You thought you needed to change
something in you, in order to find
love.
That has been a big lie
For you are love

You are love!
It is love that is opening doors for
you to many, many worlds
and many encounters of yourself.

Life is a beautiful journey.
And that journey takes you to many
places of expressing love that you
are.

Each one of your relations
are sacred,
your relationship with the
environment,
your relationship with all around you

and the most importantly, the
relationship within yourself.
That is your most sacred relation, for
it is your beautiful connection with
the one that created you,
you need you in your life, put
attention to the most sacred relation.

Love is forever
When you begin to connect
within yourself and see life through
the perception of love,
immediately you begin to increase
your own power as a human being.

By feeling love and
being love all the time,
people bring forward new ways of
expression
a new way of living through
compassion
An understanding of the
world of oneness
and the understanding
of the interconnection
with the whole.

"...it's about liberation...
it's about understanding that
you were born free.

Through your original vibration
You are very inclusive,
you comprehend that whatever is
happening to one
is happening to many,

Through your original vibration,
There is a way of thinking about
honor and respect to each other
and as a human being,
to our environment for you
understand the communication
with the whole creations,
with flowers,
trees with everything around you,
the connection with stars.
In this realm you can see yourself as
cosmic beings.
in this realm is there is the perfect
balance between the male - the
female.

*So, whatever is happening in the
inside is also happening in the
outside.
You are making the inside the same
of the outside,
and the outside the same as the
inside.*

*This perfect balance it has nothing to
do with the patriarchal system or the
matriarchal system.
No. In this world everything is about
this balance.*

*In this world you embrace the
knowing that you are love.
And you have always been love.
And through that love, you
experience a higher way of
communication
You see yourself as a bead
of information
and there is nothing to hide.*

And the communication is much more
direct for there is no more filters of,
ages, and ways of thinking,
In this realm, you embrace yourself
as a light body that you have been

There is no struggle anymore of any
kind. For you live in that entrega,
you walk in that entrega.
In that entrega, you do perceive
yourself without the filter of the
mind
or any other conflict
or identification for there is the
absence of fear.
It is the absence of destruction
and chaos.

For a while now,
you have been ruled by separation.
. People have been valuing
themselves through money,
color of the skin or background or
country.
It was the world of illusion.

The world of separation,
world of the nightmare.
The nightmare is over.

As you begin to see each one of the
steps and you begin to just look
around you and look inside of you
this incredible world,
The Golden Era, that we are just
approaching.

For a while, the guilt and shame of
the people has been bringing a lot of
distortion of love.
And love was manipulated as a
concept. But love never lost the
knowingness, a wisdom that resides
within yourself.

No matter what you see,
no matter what you do
there is always love involved.
This is the true human being.
In this world you recognize each
other
as a peaceful being by nature.

*You recognize that the freedom you
are,
the freedom you are connects
everyone in a deep manner.*

*It is not about competition anymore.
It is about understanding the visions
and experiences that you have -
that you can relate it with everyone
around you.
And the experiences are
communicating each other
but not through the struggle,
but the liberation.*

*For a while the laws of the father
have been showing what is the
difference
in every single realm as you raise
your consciousness.*

*You will begin to see incredible
understandings that you have about
yourself.
You do have help.*

Much of the assistance is
Coming from star people
and the ancient ones and many
beings all around you for the people
to raise their consciousness.

The help is that understanding
of truth and spiritual work
that human beings are doing now.

The masculine ways were clouded for
a long time,
the men could not see their divine
masculine for a while,
for only the patriarchal system was
ruling them,

Right now, they are beginning to
comprehend the love
that they have within themselves and
beginning to see the
Divine Feminine inside of
themselves.

*For she is the holy spirit, that holy
spirit that is bringing a new
revelation to all the human beings.*

*For a while now, for a woman
everything was about the world of
the form, was an obsession of the
world of the form.*

*They told you that the outside world
was the most important
for you and that was a lie.*

*The only thing that obsession with
the outside world has brought is pain
and separation
and a distortion of the identity
the way that you were looking at
yourself.*

*The world of the essence it is
completely different,
for in there it is before the creations
in there absolutely all your
conceptions of reality are taking
place*

for the possibilities,

You are living all the possibilities
right there.
And you are choosing, it is time to be
aware of your choices.

You are literally choosing to launch a
reality and that launching of a
reality will turn into a co-creation
with everyone around you.

When you are holding hands with
the Great Mother,
when you are in alignment with the
Great Mother,
the one that created you-
your purpose in life is being revealed

And when you do what
you have come here to do,
you are bringing this happiness
into your life.

Happy people create happy creations.
That incredible co-creation that
you are doing with everyone
around you,
when you are aware of
these co-creations you
will understand your responsibility
as a human being.

You are turning into a true human
being by dropping everything that
doesn't mean anything anymore.
By dropping the colonizations,
programming of separations.

You can see the programmed mind
and the lie - at the moment you
present a truth those lies
have no power anymore over you.

The understanding of that divine
feminine and divine masculine resides
within yourself.
Don't look for that balance in the
world of the form

*but in embrace that balance in this
world of the essence for this
embracing will bring you into a very
different manifestation.*

*That manifestation that comes from
that divine feminine,
from that holy spirit that you are.*

*Human beings have the
ability to recognize truth.
The love is the energy and truth is
the path and both are creating the
next step for the evolution.*

*You are part of a new reality,
of a new way of existence
and so, I am.*

So are many people around you.

*Don't fight with that 3rd and 4th
dimensional reality.
For in that fight you will get
engaged.*

That is what they want form you.
Just keep on walking in your truth
and you will see that they have no
power over you
and that is the greatest protection
and spiritual work
that you can do for your family,
your community
and for all the human beings...

"It is eminent to bring this original
vibration.
You have no idea how powerful you
are

It is powerful to comprehend the
purification times.
Human beings are going back to
innocence. Where innocence means
the original vibration, innocence is
the understanding of the balance of
the male and female, The Great
Father and the Great Mother.

Every reality is based on your belief
system - it is you the one that
perpetuate the creation,
The patriarchal system is a belief
system that was based on lies for the
many generations,
To control and enslave human beings,
yet, that system is within yourself,
the system is in you, and it is your
work to challenge those beliefs.

The System is beginning to crumble.

*It is the time of forgiveness, when
you forgive - it is a liberation that is
taking place in your heart.*

*That means that you will not operate
through revenge and hate, or you will
become what you hate the most.
I am talking about forgiving not
forgetting - you do need to remember
and recognize what is happening.*

*...As you know, your body of light is
being awakened, it recognizes the
power you have and the speed of
light.... through it, you are
recognizing that you can connect
with everyone around you,
the cosmos and you begin to realize
that you have all these helpers.
This is a beautiful planet
Your Home Gaia,
She is helping you.
Providing the next octave of the
evolution of the human being*

*You are a light body and you do
have a physical body….
I am telling you there will be a time
when everyone will be able to use
their light body…
The remembrance is way too
important right now.*

*The system wants to engage you in a
war that doesn't belong to you.
When you focus in that love,
those forces cannot get you –
the system is falling.
Let it fall.*

*We are entering into the Golden Era
and it will not be dictated by scripts
from the patriarchal system….*

*Recognizing your original vibration
that you are will make you
comprehend that you are love,
And that Love that you are will help
you to transcend*

And you know love is the most incredible powerful energy in the universe.

*Is what connects everything,
Is what integrates within yourself.*

*By letting go of the fear, separation, guilt, shame, anger –
those lower consciousness that keep on dragging you down,
you will find out that compassion will come to you in a very natural way-
like a revelation.*

There is no Feminine Ways without the sisterhood

*And now is the time
where you build the sisterhood even stronger.*

People helping people and everyone protecting the children.

That incredible love and caring that
you have,
it comes directly from your original
vibration
and it is always in alignment with
the Great Mother.

My sisters, daughters, mothers it is
the time that we begin to understand
that we are nature, and in your
nature, you know how to do this.

You know how to pass through the
purification times.
Just like the little turtles that know
how to get back to the ocean.
So are you. So, your spiritual work
has to do with believing in yourself
again.
You are a perfect being.
The enslavers make you believe that
no nobody is perfect.
Every single one of you is unique and
through that uniqueness you find
yourself. Your path is unique.

Through that uniqueness you can
understand the world of oneness.
You cannot understand the world of
oneness though a mediocrity mind.

*You can do it through your original
vibration.
Don't allow guilt, shame or even
loneliness to get in the way-
for I am telling you I am with
you. . . .
I am in you*

*Trust! Trust that you will not
sabotage or betray yourself
anymore. . .
in that way, you won't betray
anyone.
It is the time for a big awakening."*

.... there are dark forces that don't
want ascension to happen
but they can't stop it.
.... those dark forces attack by
creating false identities,
...and through those false identities
you thought you couldn't believe in
yourself...

Now is the time to believe in you...
just open your senses...
when you are able to open your
senses, your whole mind is going to
be rewired...
and these forces have no access to
your energy and have no access to
your vibration....

The bad dream of separation is
over...you live in a world of light...
all the light is interconnected and
communicating.
So are you. You are communicating
with absolutely everything around
you.

It is the time to be aware of your
own vibration, recognizing your own
vibration
It's about awareness.

Is not about the process anymore,
For you are in the times of the
quickening
Your mind wants to have that
process to feel comfortable.
When you feel the higher truths that
are available for you,
you will realize that it's not about
the limitations of the mind.

Yet, the mind is beautiful,
it's just that human beings have
forgotten how to think.
And How to use your brain.

You are into purification times.
As you call upon your light body, it is
true that all that darkness that was
hidden for a long time will be
presented.

Is true too that in the moment that
you are bringing that light,
the darkness has no power over you,
it ceases to exist.
When you bring that body of light
and you connect to your biological
body,
It is bringing so many changes
your body is being trained again to
hold that higher vibration....
every atom of your body is
remembering how to understand,
how to be that light, also in a
physical body.

In this time of the ascension you are
taking your body with you.
It might be that your body feels tired,
that you are leaving behind some
foods and craving others,
it is different for each one of you.

Embrace who you are, and remember
that body holds that nature too,
for that body is being renovated and
aligned with your light body.

*Is the time for you to trust
yourself...
for a while human beings have been
betraying themselves...
that is why you keep in secret those
things that were hurting you...
it's not about trusting others, it's
about trusting yourself...*

*As you begin to trust
you will see another kind of reality
appearing right there in front of your
eyes....
you will see...
and you will understand...
who you are as a true human
being...*

"What is raising our consciousness?
The Great Mother is inside all of you,
guiding you.
She is a voice that is not a bully,
a voice that is about the highest good
of everyone
It is a voice not judgmental or even
telling you what to do.

When you ask her, she put things in
the table for you to decide what to
do.

The only one that you need to reach
is yourself."

~ Magdala Ramirez

There is this incredible love
that you are,
that connects you to the
highest truth available for you
and living in that creates a new
perception of reality...

...that incredible triad is giving you a
new vision of who you are...
so, the old identities that
have been enslaving you for
all this time are leaving
and the connection to that essence is
bringing that integration
of your own self and
everything around you.

~ Magdala Ramirez

"I want to say to many of you
who are hesitating about your path.
Thinking 'I don't see my path clearly,
what should I do or where should I
go
and you keep on telling me to trust
myself and I don't know how to do
this'.

But I am telling you my sister, my
mothers, my daughter, my grandchild,
my son,
As you begin to walk, immediately
the path is going to appear in your
eyes.

You are the path. Your path is so, so
unique that absolutely no one
can walk it with you.
You cannot walk the path of anyone
else.

Know that, you are that path and
the walker.

Remember that in every step is your
prayer and your prayer is in every
step.
Know that when you become one
with your path,
you are being guided and you do have
the assistance that you need,
and that you also are assisting
everyone around you.

Respect the path of everyone,
for it is a soul journey and that
beautiful path that you are,
will take you to the liberation that
you have always been.
A goal, isn't really in the outside.
It's in every step. You have always
been free.
Through love you become who you
truly are because you are love."

- Magdala Ramirez

*The Sacred dance cannot happen
without the stillness,*

*The perfect orchestra is in the deep
silence.*

Put it on what you know
And bring a new manifestation
in every word that you say,
every thought, every manifestation
Make what you know a new way of
living

Remember that you are having
all the assistance you need,
Yet, it needs to be that application
Of your alignment with the one that
created you.

Don't attach to an identity,
or what they make you think you are,
for limit you to only one single
reality, enslaves you...
that was impose from the
patriarchal system to perpetuate
enslavement...
you are much more powerful...
Human beings are multidimensional
beings...
no attachments make you FLY!

"The purified heart casts no
reflection in the smoky mirror'

'You become what you connect
with...'

What it rules you now
will cease to exist
when you go into the next evolution
of yourself.

When you feel not good enough
you're not responsible either...
because you're waiting for someone
to do that for you...
to save you
thinking that
someone is going to come
in the outside and come and save you
....and in some way created an
identity about it...

The true is that no one can make the work for you. It is you the one that chooses, no one can interfere in your decision, no one can save you from you,
You are responsible of your connection with the one that created you.

When you catch yourself still thinking that way
put a guard!
...every time you are identifying with that old paradigm
you will say 'Stop!!!'
you will hear that stop ...
will require your brain...
understand that it was an automatic thing and it needs to go because it doesn't belong to you...
and you see it coming and then stop it...
name it...

Once you name it, that
energy has no power over you…
but if you hide it or identify with it,
it will have power over you

Every time you compare yourself to
someone else…
put a stop in it…
Train your mind…

*"See yourself in that nakedness
without fear"*

*"The Feminine represents the world
that is within yourself.
A world that has access to ancient
knowledge.
A world that has always been
there....*

*Is the time for you to see yourselves,
As you are
a human being as a cosmic being
and that cosmic being is about
understanding the dimensionality.*

*Human beings are truly dimensional
beings. The way that you perceive a
reality is based on your cultural
beliefs, experience in life, massive
consciousness, and also, in a very
unique form.*

The way you perceive the world is so
unique that it will be different,
even within your own family.

Each one has a different perception.
You will never know if the color blue
is the same color that everyone is
seeing.
You have concepts and definitions
inside of your head that have created
or contribute to a belief system.

Some of this belief system is
completely obsolete in this time-
space.
Yet it is creating and perpetuating a
hologram,
a dream that you have been living for
a very, very long time.

It is true that through your original
vibration,
You uncover your key and is so
unique
that no one can use that key,
only you

The ancestors left behind a
knowledge,
a path for the people to understand
the many, many worlds.
The ones that are able to embrace
balance of your female and male
energies within yourself.

Even the Christ was talking about
the kingdom of heaven,
He never said, "you have to die to get
there". He said, "it is at hand".

It is just in you. Coming back to the
key, that key is the perception of the
male -female together.

It is that uniqueness that you are,
the part of you that opens the many
worlds.

For a long time, the human beings
have been experiencing
dimensionality,
and in some cultures, it truly denied
the whole experience.
Putting the experience in a little box
and labeling it.
You can label it as 'Miracles' or as 'I
don't want to talk about it' or 'Never
talk about it'.

You might put an experience in
something that you have done before
and put it in a little box.

And in that way, it is very hard to
have an original experience because
your mind is putting absolutely that
it sees in those little boxes.

The ancestors never meant to use the
mind in that way.
They used the mind as a whole,
with no limitations.
There is no such thing as chauvinism,
separation of any kind.

When you realize that
interconnection
And that all the life forms have
within yourself,
each one with a cycle,
you can understand that you have a
cycle as a human being.

You have a cycle as a woman. You
have a cycle so unique that is you.
And you use that cycle to understand
that balance within your male and
female.
It is your very first key to enter in
what someone calls 'the fifth
dimension'.

When you as human beings,
understand that balance within
ourselves, immediately that key is
being ignited to have different kinds
of experiences.

Every single realm or world has different laws.
The laws were put there by the masculine side of god and that holds all the worlds together is the perfect harmony,
the feminine side of god.

That perfect harmony is in the essence of all the life forms.
So, you are interconnected with all the life forms and time.
Time doesn't really exist as we think of time as linear.
You can experience your real time when you are in that inner world.
Within yourself, you really are timeless.
When we are able to connect with this world,
you are literally free of time.
So, in that moment you can bend the times, for what you think past or future.

There is a rhythm or frequency that
all the life forms have.
That frequency is also based on the
frequency of your beautiful planet.
She is also part of a big cycle in the
multiverse too,
And that cycle is also interconnected
with her cycle,
and is connected with your cycle.

All the life forms happening
simultaneously.
There are doors that are being open
and closed,
that when you are in balance of your
male and female,
you enter another state,
another perception of reality.

Magdala Ramirez on 'Dimensions'
Episode

If you allow pain to dictate your life.
Then, they win.
If you allow that pain to say, "you're
not going to love again because you
got hurt",
then they win.

And it is your choice.

Remember that people in pain are
manipulable and controllable
And their creation
will be based on pain.

.

Truth is that love,
It really has nothing to do with one
person that you love or not.
It is your ability to understand and
embrace yourself through that
connection within yourself
because everyone,

Every single one that you have ever
loved in your soul journey
has taught you beautiful things
in one way or the other about love.

You did want to trust that person,
you did want to believe in that
person,
The problem was that it is really is
not about believing in that person.
It's about believing in yourself.

The problem is not about trusting
that person.
It's about trusting yourself.

This doesn't mean you need to stay
with a relation that is hurting you.
A relation that is not in that divine
order or is through a programming
meant to hurt women.
It is true that it is the time of
changes, but it starts within
yourself.

Love. Love deeply through that
connection.
Remember that every single relation
is happening within yourself.
Nothing is really lost.
Love the same way the eternal
feminine does, means absolutely no
attachment.

Walking together is a very beautiful
thing but with no attachment.
Walk into that freedom
that love is naturally,
into the purest essence of
love."

The time has come for people to
understand that
you are that portal
you are a multidimensional being.

The first portal to cross is the union
of polarities - bonding of your male-
female.

The sacred moment,
the instant you make a choice
is very powerful.
Understand when you bring the
awareness of that sacred moment,
it creates a big difference -
that choice is according to your own
vibration
or what you know about yourself.

Recognition of sacredness of life
resides within your own self
and Sacredness
will be manifested
the moment you put awareness
in your choices.

Everything is connected through the
essence.
your choices are being presented to
you
according to your vibration
that is how you are going to
choose what you want to experience.

As you begin to become more aware
of yourself, you will see how easy it
becomes to make your choices
for the highest good
for everyone.
In perfect alignment
with the one
that created you.

Your uniqueness in your path
is showing you that your goal is
being fulfilled in every step
and through hat awareness,
every step you fulfill your goal.
you fulfill who you are.

Don't allow that limitedness of your
senses to rule your life.

The experience is only that -
an experience,
and is there to show you,
to help you to understand
who you are.

Attachment of those experiences
is coming from that emotional body
that can show you a limited
perception of reality.
Use it as a stepping stone
as you are that truth and you have
many layers.
Those layers are bonded into one.
for the whole is contained in one
and one in whole.

As you begin to see the layers of all
these experiences and all these
realities that you are seeing in the
outside, you are seeing they are also
happening in the inside.

When you ask for the higher truth,
you are also seeing the higher truth
about your own self,
that will be a new way to relate
with yourself,
a higher understanding of who you
are,
a higher aspect of your own self.
It is a continual dance you have
within yourself
because the way you relate
with the outside world
is the way you are relating
with that inside world,
with the perceptions of realities
that resides within.

Remember that you are you Higher
self.
Yes, the only one that you need to
reach is yourself.

Ask for that part of yourself
to Recognize truth
and you will see the many layers...

Process is bounded by time.
But that is relative, as each human being
has a different perception of time.

Remember that the ancestors were
not measuring time
But they were measuring
Consciousness
Time is consciousness
(For now, I can tell you this.)

You can accelerate process anytime
through that awareness.
It is where that process is
being accelerated.

Open your senses.
realize what is happening
where are you,
how you are relating with that
reality,
for all what you see is inside
of you and this is how
you are relating.

What you see is a hologram
A virtual reality
that is being presented to you for
you.

Remember that fulfilling
your purpose is in every step,
the awareness of where you are
going,

And where you are
is through the presence of your own
presences
as you open your senses
all at the same time.

The awareness will happen naturally
and changes of your perception
of reality
and your choices in that sacred
moment
is how a whole new manifestation is
coming into being.
The awareness of that connection
you have, one to another, is such a
powerful understanding within
yourself because it will help you to
walk in sacredness.

You have always been sacred.
You have always been that divine
spark that comes from the creator.
It is the time to recognize
who you are.
All the relations are happening
within
yourself.
Find the other side of the mirror.
And always remember that the only
one you need to reach is yourself.
All is about alignment.

If there is fear, let it be light

if there is rejection, let it be light

if there is sadness, let it be light

if there is confusion, let it be light...

Let light be!

Is about time

Transcendence is to understand
the time in a different manner.
Time is not linear
Time is not emotion
Time is consciousness

.

"You are not bounded by time".
The ways the mother is showing you
that they are not bounded by time.
And in the way you are able to
understand the evolution is how you
will understand transcendence.

Can you empty yourself in order to be
fulfilled...?
You are a powerful woman
A powerful human being
And in you resides a great secret.
It is the understanding in your
feminine aspect that you are the Holy
Spirit.

*You hold your own enlightenment,
she is the one giving birth to the new
world, she is the one giving re-birth
to you as light, she is that realization
and awareness, for you to be able to
conceive yourself as a body of
light...*

*So, a body of light is not about
emotions nor is it a physical body,
nor is it a thought process.*

*Is very much about understanding
creation by itself,
understanding truly that you have
always been life, and not
understanding life as a series of
events like you are separated from
life.*

*Observe that part of you that is
observing at the same time who can
observe it...
who are you then...?*

You are so much higher than what
you think you are...
what you think is a tiny little bit of
what you are...
So, your thoughts can reach that
clouds and train your mind in the
cosmic way of thinking...
based on the universal
understanding...

Yes, you are life, use your body of
light, you are love.

In every cell is part of the big orchestra, in the same way goes to all your bodies - thoughts, emotions and part of that spirit that you have always been and how you are deeply connected with the higher version of yourself.

At the moment you drop an identity - Behold! don't go into another identity...
the connection is so strong that it will guiding you directly into another connection of the world not based on reality but based in a different conception of the self...

Can you understand that connection of reality?
Can you comprehend a whole new conception of the world that is all around you and inside of you...?
the love that you are will guide you directly into who you are for real and has nothing to do with identity.

*Your true reality is the one that is
happening inside of you.*

...Each one of you has your own
purpose...
no better or less...
all comes from the same life force...
that life force when you touch it and
becomes one...
you will see clearly all this identity
that you hold for comfort
will begin to drop because that is not
the parameters anymore...
You will be liberated.
You have always been Free.

Observe how a truth,
from thousands of years t
hey are still truth!

For truth has no time, truth is not
bounded by time,
neither are you
For you are truth!

The realization of connection
And multidimensionality
one contained in whole and whole
contained in one.
as well as all your bodies,
you are one and the whole at the
same time. you make that realization
through love
for you are love.
love is the connection.

Human beings are the most vulnerable of all the creations in this planet...
So, the trust needs to be there to come into this realm...
You have come to this realm to learn and living in that entrega, recognizing those experiences as experiences only, without the attachment of an identity, will help you to make the realization of yourself.

You are the life force, you have always been alive
When you recognize yourself as life, The natural choices will be for the highest good of everyone.

The programming based on separation was completely unnatural.
The inner core dictates the outside world.

It is in the inner core where you understand the life force not in the world of the form.

Make the decisions from future back, in that way you are integrating all these parts of yourself.
Connect with the one that knows how to do this, you are your Higher self.

You are part of the web.
you are part of the whole.
You are the whole
when you are raising
your consciousness
You are raising the whole web.

You are integrating yourself at the same time as you are being integrated into a higher truth of yourself.

Your true world is in the inside.
the outside world is just a hologram.

when you can see not based on
emotions but through consciousness
and frequency,
energy
you will be able to tap into the new
world

What you are vibrating is only a
tone, a note of your whole being

There is an interaction, there is a co-
creation, a song of the multiverse
where you are part of it

And through that sacred place that
you have you are also co creating
with the universe

Time to comprehend those
interactions

*All is vibrating, and sending
messages, it is you the one that
translate them in your head,
in a language that you can
understand,
accordingly
to your frequency*

*If you are able to comprehend
how those interactions are happening
you are able to comprehend the web*

*You have your unique vibration
and that is your key to the universe.
that is the song and how you are
connected.*

*Everything is interconnected, all is
bounded into one.
Everything is the web.
The point is that integrity,
that purity of your being
your possibilities, which is your web,
will be according to your frequency
range*

*Related with how much you know
you self and how much you know
your unique song, how much you
sing...
That is how the possibilities are
presented*

*...And you are aware of the
possibilities- that is divine order
...When you understand love in the
purity of expression,*

Is like you can see in yourself the tree
of life with many branches
That never ends, many possibilities
happening at the same time...

All is interrelated with everything
around you.
just like your planet is interrelated
with the constellations.
Those interrelations are the exchange
of energy, all connected of what you
can call love.

Interconnection that you have
At all times, gives you access to a
higher truth about yourself
Be aware of who you are at all times
in your original vibration,

Know who you are,
And rise your frequency
and hold the integrity of yourself.

When you understand the incredible
web, you can see in every part of
it...
time is just consciousness, which is a
frequency range...

Think about your thoughts...
thoughts are sequential.
which are a web...
one thoughts connect to one to
another...
connected to emotions...
you can affect the whole web.

And you can affect your thoughts by
creating that possibility
and understanding that possibility
according to your frequency
range is how much you know
yourself...
this can be used in every part...
even in your body...
one cell connects to
another and
another
and another...

The level of understanding
Of yourself that you have
will be in perfect
correlation of your belief system
and emotional body.
When you drop what does not belong
anymore
You will rise your
consciousnesses naturally.

Realize that there is only one root.
Imperative that is time for
reconstruction for human being.

It's the value of your encounter
about yourself from a technique, not
the value of the technique itself.

Your connection is so unique that
only you can have that.
You have a song....

Be aware of all those connections-
For in every single relation you align
naturally —
connections guided and aligned...

The realm of the feminine is the
world within yourself,
the realm where your real
teacher resides,

The realm of knowledge
and connection
is inside of you
and with everyone around you,
and the multiverse...
yes, might be that is an abstract
world,
so powerful and beautiful,
...as much truth you can handle,
as much you can embrace this world,

Just be truth in the inside
and all is being revealed...

You are a creator
For you come from Creator
True artists divinize…
the creation has a meaning….
a creation emanates love.

Ask a question and immediately
receive
an answer
…how much of the truth are you
willing to put on?

You become one with what you
desire
but not by the desire itself.
It is an energy.
. The awareness is understanding
where you are.
is about that magnetism and law of
attraction.

The information that you have about
everything around you - comes from
the world of the form,
not in the world of the essence.
Now you need to bring your
knowledge through the world of the
essence,

The purpose came through the essence
as a plan in this lifetime.
Who you are for real, comes through
the essence.
Not through the form.

Bits of information that you are translating in your brain come in a language that you can understand.

And that is part of your perception of reality of where you are.

As you love you embrace your own nature, your own nature, who you are as nature.
Love is all what it is. It is an energy all around you and inside of you, in universe, that uniqueness you have.
See it as an energy ... everything is entirely connected inside of it you are able to perceive that connection you are inside of you.
It is in your spirit. That incredible connection within yourself – not just in your lifetime, or this 'present',
You can't communicate with great mother without love,

You are a community by nature. You
are sisters by nature. You have been
into the code of honor or feminine
and masculine. This happens in a
way that is natural. You won't
betray your sister.

Love the understanding and
understand love.

When you realize,
you won't resist the change…

The Mother cannot give you
anything you cannot put it on.

Do not cry for the things that have
gone because you denied me

Do not attach for the things that
doesn't exist because you reject me

I am the one who fulfill you
And to empty you
And fulfill you again

I am the pulse of the universe
And all is within me
I am you

Show me the lullaby that comes from
the stars
So, I can remember who I am

Show me the lullaby that comes from
the spring
So, I can remember where I am

Show me the lullaby that comes from
the flowers
So, I can remember the beauty in me

Show me the lullaby that comes from
the mirror
That when I see you...I see me...

Beautiful song that the Great
Mother gave us in moon dance
ceremony

Yo soy tu

Magdala

Here I am! In my presence in this
realm, I have been in silence for such
a
long time, for a while you couldn't
recognize me, you didn't know about
me,

I have always been here... waiting
for this time...

Yes, I am the light and your truth, I
am the giver of light, it is through
me where light comes forth, and the
time has come for the revelation,
what
it was hidden now is in the light,

I am the eternal Feminine, I am love,
the beginning and end, I am the one
that fulfill you, the one that empty
you, and fulfill you again.

I am the one that unites and
separates, the one that heals, the one
that open your

eyes, I am the revelation...

Your beautiful planet is in many
changes... Human beings are in many

changes, and in each revelation is
another step of the pyramid,
awakening

your immeasurable power,
for your love bounded into one

I am the Mother and the Daughter, I
am woman, I am life, I am light,
I am
Your truth...
I am the eternal feminine,

*Many seeders have come to your
planet for many ages, many
civilizations,*

*they have come from many higher
realms creating the path for the many
world,*

*and now is the time of the harvest
again, as many of you know, they are
many*

*entrance to those worlds where the
perfect vibration within yourself,
holds*

*the key to enter, I am asking you to
go to those worlds and hold that*

vibration for the many.

Sacredness is everywhere...

Do not fear me my brother, my father, my lover... for it is me who gives

you light and life. I gave birth to you twice. It is through me where your

light is coming from. Now it is the time that you support the light givers, for

it is me the one that speaks through them. You! the seeder, know that I am

always with you.

Do not fear me my sisters, my daughters, my mothers, for it is me the one

that has brought to you the revelation. I am the one who reveals

your sacredness, who knows that all around you and inside of you resides in

sacredness, see in your brothers and fathers and lovers the true man, for it

is me the one that gave them life, for I am the mother of all the living

things.

I am the perfect vibration that awakes, heals, reveals. I am the path and the walker. In me resides many worlds, I am the door!

I hold the times in my hand, for I am not bounded by time, Know me!

For I am you!

Making Heaven of Earth and Earth on Heaven

...There is the self, and the one that is connected with all around, personal and impersonal, subjective and objective, ... there are one and the same...
see the things for the highest good of everyone, and relate in that way, a whole shift in you, at the same time that you can see your own self, your own self is included in the highest good of everyone, is like a realm, when is not personal or impersonal anymore... only an energy that exist in all realms, have access to all realms, and contains the whole.

...The time and spaces, all are happening together, a new way of emotion is emerging in some way or another, a time, where you are all the relations, and all spaces... nothing really matters, only that

.... *Witnessing, vibrating, in a so subtle manner, connecting, uniting, integrating, within a kind of "you" that doesn't exist, I kind of self where all is related, a sublime force, that guides, direct, complete in some way...*

.... *A place where only balance exists, and a path where is much more than that, a realization that nothing exists without balance, nothing matters just that, an eternal perpetual understanding... where love, shape shift to a higher perspective*

A portal awakes inside of you, a new perception of a reality is being embrace...

Con Mucho Amor

Yo soy tu

Magdala

About the Author

Magdala Ramirez
Spiritual Leader. Healer. Priestess.
Author. Teacher

Magdala Ramirez Garcia is a spiritual leader and healer from the Maya Mexika lineage. She was born as medicine woman, from a long linage of medicine people, in Mexico where she began walking her path at an early age working with the medicine people and the pyramids of Mexico.

She brings the ancient knowledge to the world through original seminars, books, ceremonies, and journeys.

Magdala's purpose in life is to bring back the ancient wisdom of the union of the polarities, and through this wisdom she helps to bring back the perfect balance of the male and female.
She is the founder of many ceremonies including Moondance, Priestess, The 144: Giving Birth to a New World, and The 13 hours of Drumming.

She has led Vision Quests, and Journey's to Sacred Places to share the knowledge. When she is not traveling for ceremonies or seminars, she is working to bring forth valuable information through her books, her school of Ascension and her radio show.

Magdala is author of many books that speak about the ancient wisdom of the feminine including, "I am You", "Story of Quetzalcoatl", "World of the Enchanted Flower",

"Sacredness of the Union of Polarities", "Sacred Sex", "The 13th Mirror", "The Teachings of the Crystal Skulls", "The Triad of the 13 Mirrors", "Earth on Heaven", and "Moon Codex", "Eternal Feminine, Wild Woman". As well as creating books, Magdala has developed unique, interactive tools to help people work within themselves. These tools include Aztec Runes and the Games of the Goddess.

She is the Founder and Executive Director of Sacred Woman, a non-profit organization devoted to helping women realize their highest potential.
She is a founder of Online School of Ascension, where you can join any time

For more information you can visit Magdala's website at www.magdalas.com or www.sacredwoman.org. You can

listen to her weekly radio show
where she is speaking with many
leaders of the feminine everywhere in
the world at
http://www.blogtalkradio.com/sacre
dwomanorg.
Her email is Quetzalkina@gmail.com
You can also write to her to
Po box 1151
El Prado NM
87529

69752136R00089

Made in the USA
San Bernardino, CA
21 February 2018